Debra

As the world rotates, so do our lives)!

Barnett

Kaleidoscope

by E. J. Barnett

Strategic Book Publishing and Rights Co.

Strategic Book Publishing and Rights Co.
12620 FM 1960, Suite A4-507
Houston, TX 77065
www.sbpra.com

ISBN: 978-1-61204-834-5

Book Design: Suzanne Kelly

This book is dedicated to God
My creator, my shield, and my guide

To my mother for encouraging me to trust my feelings
And to believe in their magic for healing.
To my brother, Toby, for paving the way
For his eleven sisters and his brother.

Foreword

Kaleidoscope captures the essence of our being as we endeavor in our journeys through life.

Ms. Barnett allows us to see and experience the beauty of life at its finest. We feel the joy, the pain, the disappointments, and achievements, all bits and pieces rotating in harmony.

No demons are hidden in crevices; no heroes go unnoticed. Instead, they are all brought forward into the light as the kaleidoscope continues its ever constant rotation.

Kaleidoscope peers into all facets of life. It allows us to see what we want to see, though we realize that it's an ever-changing scenario.

Thank you, Emily, for this most provocative insight.

—Yvonne Craver, sister

Life

E. J. Barnett

Clay

Babies are God's clay to man
To mold, to shape,
To present the masterpiece
Back to God.

Simplicity

Take time
To relinquish the struggles
Of the mind.

Drift into the world
Of your imagination
And dream.

Pursue the life
Most sought,
No doubts, no fears

But with blinders,
And live the creation
Of your dreams.

E. J. Barnett

Pregnancy

I have lain down
With the intent of seeding,
Choosing the proper time
My nectar would be ripe
For pollinating.

I have felt you swim
In the river of life,
Unfolding, preparing
To enter my world
Attached only by a vine.

Waiting the anxious
Moments life has set aside,
The embryo completing
Its cycle, disrupting
My thoughts.

Pushing, groaning, grunting,
Hurting, screaming,
Watching, listening, smiling,
Knowing my seed has opened
Into a life all its own.

The Addicts

I cannot tell you of its birth,
Only of its life and its death.
There were three of them, two girls, one boy,
They each had their own accompaniment;
For the eldest, it was her hair.
Before the craving began, she had bangs.
The hair was pulled over the nose and the lips;
There was a sensation that was needed to soothe,
Perhaps only a psychologist could tell why
The touch was needed over the nose and lips.

The other needed her blanket.
It was held tight between the fingers,
Yet, caressing the ear, the cheek, and the lip.
The size was not important,
Nor was the state of its hygiene,
Only the blanket, the same blanket.
Once it was misplaced and another given,
Rejection was followed as the craving began.
The screaming, the scratching, and the hitting of her own face,
Drawing blood, but no pain, only the craving.

He used a finger as his companion,
It too, was held against the face,
Wrapping itself securely around the nose,
As he picked at the second joint with his other hand,
Until there was a callus that grew with age.
Each time the withdrawals began,
He became quiet and settled into a chair,
Each hand was needed to soothe.
There was little or no talking until
Relaxation, security, and peace were restored.

Each, shared their troubled times, those times that were
Bearable when they had what they needed most.
Habits were not destroyed, though attempts were many,
Some with carefully placed pepper,
Some had hands tied, during the night,
Some were forbidden privileges, or bribed with more.
Some were mocked and teased,
They succumbed to nothing,
Their need was too great.

One day, the eldest, took on a challenge,
Thirty days must pass.
She found herself nauseous
From the craving and she was often irritable.
On the twenty-ninth day, in her sleep, she found relief.
The discovery was made in the wee hours,
She cried, having failed and knowing the cost,
An addict forever, she would be.
Having gone twenty-nine, to her challenger, she had won.
The others marveled at her success,
And sucked their thumbs no more.

Happy Birthday

Another year to salute
The passing of time,
Treasured memories, and
Coveted moments in life
That I crave, just knowing
You're still passing time
In my secret world.

E. J. Barnett

Freedom

Again and again,
Hurdling obstacles
To catch the fleeting moments,

Chains, locks, ropes,
The remnants in the distance,
As a butterfly, it flutters.

Languishing in joy
As it seeps through the cracks
Defeating wasted lives.

Winifred

Orthodox mom, wife,
Baking, planting, creating
Motherhood, wifehood.

E. J. Barnett

Time

Time passes quickly,
Deceiving the hesitate;
Grasp the moment.

Live, do not linger;
The confused, the undecided,
Is lost in time.

Decisions in haste,
Defying of terror,
Living, defeating time.

The Three Little Pigs

Come, my children, you're leaving home;
Remember with what to build your houses.
If straw, a strong wind will destroy it.
Without morals, you have nothing to build upon.

Remember, you must have something
Stronger than sticks or wood.
You will be destroyed if you elect to drift;
You must take charge and choose your life.

It is stone or brick that is best, solid and firm.
You will have spiritual guidance,
Family values, and mentally alert
To select your own path.

You, my eldest daughter, are moving
To the west, to a city filled with wolves, foxes,
And others that will see you as prey,
Anxiously awaiting your arrival; design your shelter well.

My sixth child, you are leaving for an airborne career.
You too will become the quest of many fierce creatures.
While flying about, gather many stones to build your home.
Listen well; each stone has a tale.

My second son, the military has claimed your life.
Wars will devour you, if you become driftwood.
Plant yourself firmly in a mind of stone,
And flee the maggots of the land.

E. J. Barnett

Come, let me hug you, let me squeeze you,
Let me give you my love and my spirit within
To guide you, to protect you, to comfort you,
To your home, your heart, and your soul.

They Mock Me

I smile,
There are those who say too often,
There are those who say too broadly,
I listen, not knowing why
A smile is weighed for its existence.

I smile,
Those who work with me ask why,
Laboring in public, serving the masses,
I am paid a fair amount for my performance.
Should I give less than I receive?

I smile,
There are those who reflect their visions,
The grin of the Cheshire cat.
I observe what I see,
Reveling in the merriment being portrayed.

I smile,
There are those who see joy and happiness and think too
    shallow,
I give to them what you give to me.
I give you my pain and sadness,
You give me my smile.

Depression

When he greets you, his presence is often welcomed.
You are alone, your mind wandering to places and events that
    are history.
He encourages those memories, pointing out the dark secrets,
Allowing you to linger over questionable times, those most
    confusing.
Was I driving too fast? I was well within the limit.
Was I not listening when she spoke? I loved our conversations.
Did I not hear the baby crying, monitor on, the house silent?
Did I not touch him? Did he not know that I loved him?

With each greeting, he comforts more and takes more.
He decides the foods you eat, or perhaps sleeping instead of
    eating.
He offers you a drink to relax you and leaves the bottle close.
He smiles, as he walks to the phone to deaden it, the noise.
Time passes; your house becomes your town; your bed, your
    home.
Day or night, it matters not, the sun is forbidden to enter.
Water closets, annoying but necessary, mirrors passed without
    reflections.
These are the moments; he has yet to conquer, the light, the
    image, the innocent.

He embraces you, cuddles with you, sleeps with you.

Each time you leave his bed, he has a gift awaiting your return.

First a colt from the early twenties, a collector's item, in mint
condition.

A rope made of the finest hemp, presented as a lasso.

In your hand he places a bottle filled with a rainbow of colors,
beautiful colors.

You caress and cling to each, passing the privy, this time,
viewing the reflection.

Oh! The horror! Crumbling to the floor, as the dam breaks
inside, healing the pain.

Faintly, a knock at the door, sunlight peeks beneath the drapes.

E. J. Barnett

The Great Rape

We met hundreds of years ago,
When you fell in love with me,
And decided to take me to your home
Against my free will.

After being around you awhile,
I began to like you, to copy you.
I decided to talk like you, walk like you,
And even to look like you.

Curly I straightened,
Black I bleached,
Christianity I vowed,
Gods be God?

Thousands of years ago,
It was me alone,
Ruler of all lands
Free was my will.

I carved, painted, built
Great cities, temples, homes.
I moved with the earth.
I felt so natural, so real, so beautiful, so me.

Curly and straight, I knew the skill of both.
Blackness, I dominated; it was supreme.
My gods, I served well, favored none,
God is my gods?

Today we pass one another,
Often without glance or speech.
I'm going back thousands of years;
You're going back hundreds.

I speak, paint, build,
I'm greater than my father's teacher;
My father's father was his teacher.
For a moment, I let you teach, you knew not how.

I create from the creator's creations,
I'm everything there is, I'm Black!
I pray for rain, for sunshine, for beauty,
Each god answers, primitive?

The Butterflies

Lightly, fluttering,
Flicking his wings,
Playing with the rhythm of my hands,
Urging me on.

Yellow spots,
Soft wings of yellow spots,
Black velvet body,
Lurching away from my grasp.

I haven't seen you in such awhile.
For a moment, I thought your cycle complete,
But nature is still in balance.
Perhaps, it's man.

Non-Revenue

He's being paged,
He's excited,
He creeps forth
To accept his ticket
For passage.

His body slithers unnoticed
Through the crowds,
Fearing the discovery
Of his existence
To travel.

Searching silently for a corner
To crawl, to make his coil,
Maintaining the heat of his body,
Asking for nothing,
But hoping.

The aroma of food
Has awakened his nostrils,
Perhaps a morsel will fall,
He must lunge unnoticed
Or suffer visibility.

At last, the trip has ended,
He waits for all to leave,
He slithers from his corner,
Sheds his skin, stands tall,
Grateful for another journey.

Retribution

It is a day of retribution,
Going down memory lane,
Lifting the fallen branches of
Tormented souls of the past;
Shaking the bushes in
Search of the hiding unkempt secrets
That have been lurking in the
Shadows, waiting for the moments
To expose the rumors and whispers.
Forgive me.

I can share the blame with others
Only to continue a shallow
Request that has lived for so long
In my mind, keeping me
Pretending to be happy. Blocking
The entrance to memory lane, only
Stopped the images long enough to
Create creeping vines in search
Of new crevices of escape.
Forgive me.

Today, lifting branches, shaking bushes,
I inhale the dust, the excrement,
The pain, the anguish, the disappointment,
The ugliness of yesterday and my sorrow.
Humbly I ask of you,
Please forgive me.

I see remnants of the
Freshly baked cookies, filled
With the most powerful cannabis
Found in the area. You
Enjoying every bite before taking your
Journey home. The tortured drive
Filled with hallucinations and painfully
Praying to end this journey in safety.
Though your prayers were
Granted, the demons remained to
Haunt; they came to me and
Gleefully danced in circles, repeating
Your venture, deciding to remain with me.
Please forgive me.

Solitude

Though silent,
I know I'm not alone.
You are with me,
Though you do not intrude.

I Believe in Make-Believe

I believe in make-believe.
As a child, I was told there was a man
Who came each year and gave presents
To all the good children in the world.
As a child, I was told a king was born.
People were happy; they came from all lands, bringing gifts.
Perhaps, the man gives presents,
To remind us of the birth of the King.

I believe in make-believe.
As a child, there was a bunny
That came each year and left eggs
Of many colors throughout the land.
As a child, I was told that a King died.
He died so each of us might have a new birth.
Perhaps the eggs of many colors are to remind
The people of the world of a new birth, a new life.

I believe in make-believe.
As a child, I was told of knights and damsels,
Love would come from a look, a touch, a kiss,
Perhaps that is why the heart is hidden.
We must first seek, then embrace, then give,
It is then the heart opens and enfolds love.
I believe in make-believe!

The Retiring Flight Attendant

Months, years, decades,
Soaring far above the earth,
Serving thousands, mentoring few.
Promises, challenges, wishes fulfilled,
Adieu! Adieu! It's time, adieu!

Drifting slowly, back to the beginning,
Yearning for peace, solitude, quiet utopia,
Memories upon memories, releasing
Thoughts of history, remembering
Smiles of progress in soaring.

Tears of joy departing,
Departing flights of decades.

Love

Serenity

Sitting,
Watching the rays of the morning sun
Spread her luster over the immaculate horizon,
Preparing the earth for a kaleidoscopic arrival.

Sitting,
Listening to the singing of the birds,
Each in complete unrehearsed harmony,
Flying, creating a majestic tapestry.

Sitting,
Smelling the aromas of enchanting flowers,
The morning glory, the seductive rose, the shy mum.
Inhaling sights unseen, sounds unheard.

Sitting, watching, listening, smelling,
Beauty, music, amorous delights.
The alpha, the omega.

The Catcher

He comes ever so often
And takes away with him
Those that aren't labeled.
He was here today.

In his cage, there was one
A bit like you.
Howling, barking, and scratching,
Yet the doors remained barred.

If he comes again,
He may take you away from me.
No label I have to give.
Don't howl; my love is your freedom.

Moments

Today, yes!
Tomorrow, no promises.
Today, yes!
Let us live today.

Friendship

I had thoughts of you today,
Often they come, they pass,
Not today, they chose to live.

Cradling moments of time past,
We talked, we laughed, about what?
The blending of spirits, unbridled and free.

Lazily glancing at the marvels of nature,
Clouds dancing, flowers waving
Embracing the wind as friends.

E. J. Barnett

Shar-On

What an odd place to find you
Or you me,
In the mist of aerial affairs
Until the setting sun.

What an opportunity
To dwell from house to house
And have you create
The beauty of your soul
Shar-On.

Thoughts of You

It's raining;
My nose is pressed
To the window.
It's cold;
My face is distorted.
I'm smiling at you.

E. J. Barnett

Intimacy

Some need gaiety
Some need silence,
It is in sharing
Harmony is achieved.

Memories

I passed wild flowers today
And thought of you.
Remember when we played in the fields
Surrounded by beautiful colors?
Friends forever! Remember?
I miss you.

E. J. Barnett

Miss CC

She sits priestly,
Smiling, listening, observing
Those in audience,
Speaking winsomely when invited.

Words are just,
Malice is a stranger to
Her cryptic tongue,
Savoring moments of lusty wisdom.

She sits priestly,
Holding, caressing, fondling,
Each sound, each gesture,
Loving those in audience.

The Pearl

Most ancient of all gems
Yet time has not dulled her luster,
Her pure undaunted beauty.

There are many, often side by side,
Yet twins do not exist.
Unique, magical, treasured by the innocent.

The gem of love, of romance,
Reflecting the moon's brilliance
As she cradles the sacred souls.

E. J. Barnett

My Bouquet

My sisters, my sisters
Each of you is so special,
Each of you is so different,
So in tune with your spirit,
So free, so alive, so beautiful,
You are my bouquet.

Some of you are my gladiolas.
Each time I see you, we share
A new adventure with unbridled excitement.
Provoking moments of mischievous pleasures.

Some of you are my tulips,
I come to you with my fears, my pain,
You are strong, steadfast, and comforting.
Consoling without surprises, unwavering, planted.

Some of you are my roses.
We grow together, evolving,
Creating memories as we peel away our youth.
Unveiling pain, pleasures, and secrets to their futures.

My sisters, my sisters
Each of you is so different,
So in tune with your spirit,
I feel so radiant, so special, so beautiful,
Thank you for embracing me,
A grateful dandelion.

The Maiden Voyage

One and five years ago,
I decided it was time to take the voyage.
I waited to share the event with my knight,
To enjoy the entire journey, before entering the forest.
It was not to be.

I chose another,
Though I did not know he was unprepared
To take me into the enchanted forest as a knight;
He had never been with a maiden, and much was unknown.
Patience and a map were needed to explore the forest.

The journey was rough, as though it was not meant to be.
There were detours, there was confusion, and there was pain,
    great pain.
There was tension, there was conversation,
Describing the path that should be taken,
Yet it mattered not, the traveler remained lost, as I remained
    detached.

Others have taken this voyage,
Many with their knights.
Many without maps, without pain, for the journey was known,
The forest beckoned for the knights to come,
To explore the beauty that was within.

E. J. Barnett

We entered, though not together,
The traveler chose to present me to the forest
As though I was his to give.
He was excited that he entered without a map,
It was cold, dark, unenchanting, fearful.

There are those who warn against traveling with strangers,
Without your chosen knight.
There will be haste, discomfort, impatience, and some abandon
After entering the forest, leaving seeds, but no trails to follow.
Some become ruthless.

I entered without my knight. It was not a pleasant journey,
Yet I was not abandoned.
I did not find the forest enchanting.
I often thought of it, and the knight that would guide me.
One day he came, and we entered the Enchanted Forest
    together.
It was spellbinding!!

Whispers

Come, sit with me.
Tell me of your dreams, your pleasures.

Come, dance with me.
Twirl me around and around;
Make me drunk with gaiety.

Come, lie down with me.
Tell me of your life as you hold me.

E. J. Barnett

The Children

Some called her Ruby,
Some called her Ruby Lee,
I called her Mama,
She answered to all.

She grew up alone,
There were no brothers,
There were no sisters,
She was alone and often lonely.

Forty-five years ago, she had a son,
Forty-three years ago, she had a daughter,
The years passed, children flourished,
Today she has thirteen.

She bought glasses for each child,
They were beautiful rose-colored glasses.
The children wore them when venturing out,
The children embraced the world in their
Rose-colored glasses.

She smiled,
Knowing her children
Were happy.

I Love You

You have questioned my love,
Doubting the words measuring their depth.
You have questioned my love,
Wanting declarations and affirmations.

When I consume the nectar of summer fruits,
Perfect, sweet, and juicy,
It is because of you,
The pleasure is enhanced to ecstasy.

When I leave at dawn for an early run,
The sun still hiding beyond the horizon,
It is because of you,
My run is miles of timeless joy.

When I lie in your arms,
While you read to me,
It is because of you,
The sound soothes and embraces.

When I sit alone,
Thanking God for my day,
It is because of you,
I sit alone expressing my gratitude.

When our bodies entwine,
The juices dripping from the moment,
It is because of you,
The union is in harmony.

E. J. Barnett

Do not question what is,
Love is in living and in giving.
I cannot declare what God has bestowed,
But it is because of you that I share.

Four Seasons

Remember when the leaves turned?
When the green became yellow,
The yellow orange,
Orange brown.

Remember when the snows began?
When the rains froze,
The grass withered,
Flowers died.

Remember when the winds culled?
When the clouds danced,
The dust flew,
Plants budded.

Remember when the sun was bright?
When the nights were long,
The stars twinkled,
We met.

A Lass, a Maiden, a Dowager

Have you ever run for a bus, and it left you?
I have.
I ran fast and hard, alone, not caring but catching.
The door closed as I approached.
The driver drove away as I tapped on the window.
Others standing, waiting for other buses, seemed to pity me.
One spoke, "How merciless."
Amused, yet words remained thoughts,
Grateful for rejection.
Life is far too valuable to be in the hands of one so callous.

Have you ever designed a candlelight dinner for yourself?
I have.
I chose all my favorite foods, the freshest, the ripest, and the
    sweetest.
The table was set with the most exquisite linen.
Candles were chosen by size, by shape, by color.
Entering my closet, seeking the perfect dress,
Something sensuous, velvet, something uninhibited, short, very
    short.
I felt spunky and naughty.
My eyes took in the setting I chose.
My tongue savored each morsel as it was presented.

Have you ever gone to a movie or the theater, alone?
I have.
Walking down the aisle, seeking the perfect seat,
Sitting, watching the stage before the performance,
Turning briefly, as others enter, searching,
Smiling at those sitting as neighbors,
Inviting pleasantries, but little conversation,
Reading the program and watching the trailers,
Applauding the moment the lights go dim,
Bursting with excitement for the magic ahead.

Have you ever made love to yourself?
I have.
Stripping before the mirror,
Allowing my eyes to linger slowly over my body,
Delicately stepping into a warm, scented bath,
Caressing each sacred crevice as I wash,
Gently drying and selecting the perfect oil to clothe my damp
    body,
Rubbing gently as I linger, to awaken all senses,
Smiling as I feel the pleasures within,
Then donning the softest robe, draping my body to seal the
    moment.

E. J. Barnett

Have you ever taken a vacation alone?
I have.
Plans were not made for hotels or transportation,
Decisions were made for participating, not spectating,
Running, hiking, biking, and perhaps conversation in passing.
I took a plane, a train, and even a bus
Hiking mountain terrain, seen by few,
Running in towns without races,
Biking from village to village, accepting greetings
As the natives extended themselves to the lone traveler.

Have you ever been lonely amongst friends and in a crowd?
I have.
Achieving the final run in a neighborhood softball game,
Accepting the cheers and enjoying the hugs,
Window shopping with favorite girlfriends,
Breaking only for a light lunch,
Partying and dancing to the wee hours,
Conversing with friends, solving the world's problems,
Sharing a kiss that is only a kiss,
It's lonely going out, when there is so much within.

Insoon

Insoon, she is called,
Those that mock
Know not what lies within
Beyond the eyes, beyond the smile
The spirit unlocked
Free as the wind in spring.

Insoon, she is called,
Dancing to the beat
Of different drums,
Laughing in rhythm
With the humming bird
Floating on the wings of time.

Insoon, she is called,
Chasing dreams without fear,
Steady she trods,
The paths unplotted,
Running to greet her destiny,
With her eyes, her smile, her rhythm.

E. J. Barnett

It's a Girl

There were times I thought of children,
Giving birth and watching the stages of time
Through the crawling, the walking, the talking.
The thoughts remained as they were, undisturbed
By the passing of time, the absence of yang,
Until the call, the unexpected call.

I listened well,
The time had come, much was needed.
First, the diapers, many, carefully choosing the proper size,
The bed, with rails to protect, but not confine.
A wardrobe, easy to get in, easy to get out,
Most important, the changing, the feedings, and patience.

Stunned, disbelieving, even frightened,
My work, my schedule, is it possible?
I would need help; there's more than preparing a room,
Yet, fondly gazing at the perfect bed, the soft lighting,
The hair brush, the night garments, and the dresses,
I knew I was ready for my girl, my beautiful girl.

As I welcomed her home, she was quiet.
I spoke of her room and then about her past.
She smiled as I spoke of history.
She too began to talk, to laugh, to sparkle.
We disrobed, then dressed for our first night together,
Joyously, watching her choose what to choose.

She sat on her bed; I sat opposite.
We talked, time passed, she said goodnight.
Carefully pulling the covers, I adjusted the rails,
As I leaned over to kiss her goodnight, fighting the tears
     within.
Lingering at the door, allowing my mind to drift to my youth,
When it was I, who was the girl.

As time passed, she wanted to visit friends,
Friends that God chose years ago.
We dressed; I drove, often changing direction
As she changed her mind, much like that of a two-year-old.
We stopped for ice cream, we sometimes window shopped,
We forgot we were visiting friends, rather she did.

One morning, while sitting at breakfast,
She was quiet. There was an odor; I knew it well.
Walking to the bathroom, embarrassment in her eyes,
I tried to soothe. "I love these moments, when I can bathe you,
As you once bathed me." Smiling, I saw a new look,
One of love, of warmth; we hugged and she held tight.

Make-up time was another venture, lipstick
Covering more than her lips, and her wig slightly tilted.
Help was given as she dressed for dinner, or was it church?
It mattered not the occasion, only the moments were important.
"Where are we going?" "I need to go to the grocery store."
"Where did you say we were going?" I smile, I drive, I let her
     talk.

E. J. Barnett

It's been six months; we had two years.
There were those who said it would be hard. "Why?"
There were those who chose to stay away, which was okay.
I chose to be with my mother, to feed her, to wash her body,
And I listened as she repeated the stories over and over, just as
    a child.
I kissed her when she was frightened, knowing her mind
    wandered,
Her bladder was weak and at times, she said I was a nice lady.

Sometimes, I sit and cry, having had such a short time.
As I brushed her hair, she told me that she loved me.
When I bathed her, she asked why hadn't I married.
When sitting in her room reading to her, she said,
"I know you could have put me somewhere, but you didn't."
I left her room crying; how could I give up my girl,
When my girl chose to keep me?

Rituals

My hands are so cold.
She walks, stalking and sniffing;
My feet are so wet.

I want to leave her,
I want the comfort of warmth,
But I must remain.

Surgery is needed,
The tendons are ripped, destroyed
Arthritis ruling.

The winds are so strong,
Blowing harshly against me,
She sniffs, spins, turns, squats.

It's nearly over,
The winds have ceased, calm, putrid,
Relieved, happy, cold.

Legacy

Bon Voyage

The doctors have left little hope,
The heart is tired, the lungs collapsing,
The white corpuscles are being destroyed,
The lump in his stomach is growing.
      He Smiles

"Give me your hand," he tells his wife.
"Listen well; it's about time for me to take a trip.
I won't need too many things,
But I want a big farewell party.
Tell the kids I want them in their best.
Call all my friends; here's my book.
Tell them I want gifts for my trip,
Nothing big and fancy, just something with some thought."
      He Smiles

Tears are flowing as Grandpa continues,
"Stop all that nonsense; nothing's to spoil my celebration.
I've been in this bed much too long for gloom;
I'm excited about my gifts, my feast, and my trip.
Someone told me, I'm going to paradise.
The birds, the lions, and even the fish
All dwell together in the air, on land, and sea.
I've gotta see that for myself."
      He Smiles

"Everything must be true,
No one has ever come back.
That's for me, a paradise that's so grand,
No one wants to come back to tell about it."
  He Smiles

We all prepare for Grandpa's party.
Mama cooks all his favorite foods,
Nana calls all his friends and family,
Daddy goes out to buy a present.
Grandpa leaves the hospital for home.
The guests are gathered and the gifts are many.
He opens them, one by one.
He lingers over each.
  He Smiles

Daddy gives him a bottle of brandy.
Grandpa peers at him slyly.
He smells the brandy, then becomes serious,
"Take care of my baby and all these young'uns,
Paradise or no paradise, if you neglect them,
I'll be back, dat burn you," and they embrace.
Daddy says to Grandpa, "Stop worrying;
Have a nice trip, you old kook."
  He Smiles

Mama comes forward with her gift.
Grandpa's eyes betray him; she places
His hand on her belly, "Daddy, your line
Continues." He kisses her belly.
  He Cries

E. J. Barnett

Aunt Myrtle steps forward to lighten the party,
"My favorite brother," her card reads,
A carving knife and fork, "a chef is a chef,
Whether here or there." Grandpa holds them upright.
"I'm going to paradise to relax, not work,
But I suppose no one carves the way I carve.
I can never have anything done for me;
I've got to do it myself to have it done right."
	He Smiles

Toby, the eldest of his grandchildren,
Slowly stands before him and presents his gift.
Grandpa opens the box; he holds up a brown stocking cap.
His eyes cloud, they embrace, Toby won't let go.
"You're mine; you've always been mine,
But I want you to help your grandmother, your mother, and
	your sisters
Do all the things I wanted to do—travel the world, taste the
	wines,
Partake of the land, then come, I'll be waiting."
	He Cries

I come to Grandpa with twelve roses, one bud, and fifty cents.
The money is a debt being paid,
The bud is for Mama's unborn, and
The twelve roses for love from the grandchildren being left
	behind.
	He Cries

Nana gives Grandpa a small box, beautifully wrapped.
He slides the box into his pocket.
There are many rumors as to her gift,
But decades of memories and love can only be shared by the
    two.
        He Holds Her Tight.

Gifts are still coming and friends still laughing,
Then the limousine appears at the peak of festivities.
It is long and pink with beautiful silk drapes.
Grandpa swiftly walks to his elegant car.

We all stand and watch as he sits inside,
Some wave, some smile, and some cry.
He looks like a king sitting on a throne,
Having merriment with his subjects before moving on.

We all watch till he is out of sight.
There is silence, then a bit of conversation.
Nana says, "A toast, today is a happy occasion,
My husband received all his earthly rewards while living."

I was eleven at the time,
I look forward to paradise.
Grandpa promised he would return if disappointed,
And now I'm thirty-two and excited about my trip.

A Mother's Masterpiece

Weep not, for he is not gone,
Though you cannot caress his skin,
Hold his body close, or tousle his hair,
As you did when greeting him after school,
As you did while watching him study in the quiet hours.

Weep not, for you have done well,
Your son's life was not too short, just long enough.
Long enough to help those in need of comfort,
Long enough to love without boundaries,
Long enough to see the beauty in the seasons.

Weep not, for he has merely taken a walk,
A walk to explore the world beyond the mountains,
A walk to soothe the souls of other mothers,
A walk to sit with lonely friends,
A walk to pass on to all he touched, his company,
A walk to greet other sons and daughters.

Weep not; it is a time to rejoice.
Stand tall, head high, walk proud,
You bore a son that became a man,
Physically blessed, mentally gifted, yet a single man,
Compassion unbridled, patience untapped,
Sensitive to the thoughtless and grateful to the thoughtful.

Life

Don't weep,
Not for me, not for us,
As the flowers bloom,
The trees bud,
It is life, moving on.

E. J. Barnett

Ma Pierce

Three years ago, she had a party.
We all came, my family, her family, her friends.
It was her ninety-seventh birthday,
She laughed, danced, and sang "Happy Birthday" to herself.

She's too old to continue in her profession.
Many have said she is fighting senility.
Perhaps she is old, perhaps her mind does wander,
It wasn't always so, not when she was a midwife.

My twelve siblings and I were all birthed at home.
Daddy was nervous with each of us.
Mama, in her bed, waiting for Ma Pierce.
She would arrive like a storm, shouting and making demands.

Children were not allowed mischief,
The only time the roaches tipped around.
The waiting was unbearable, but we knew when it was over,
Daddy would open a bottle of whiskey and get two glasses.

Ma Pierce would drink her whiskey and instruct us.
"I don't want you disturbing your mama.
She's tired; it's been a long night.
The baby is beautiful, another girl. One boy and seven girls."

Eighteen months later, it happened again.
We were silent, the whiskey ready and waiting.
Ma Pierce came out smiling, Daddy got all the glasses,
He called all the neighbors, opened six bottles of whiskey, it's
    a boy.

Ma Pierce came four more times.
We knew the procedure well.
Daddy always had the whiskey,
But it was always two glasses, one for him and one for her.

There were many others that she birthed,
About one hundred and sixty related to me.
They were all at the party,
Three hundred more, I never knew.

Time passes quickly, winter arrives,
The bones are not soft, but quite brittle.
The mind reminisces, often thinking of spring and summer,
Sometimes wanting to remain in summer.

"Let me see a hundred and I'll be happy,"
My husband, always willing to please,
Embraces Ma Pierce and says, "Ma Pierce, you'll see a
    hundred."
She smiles and says, "Thank you, hon, but you ain't God."

Ma Pierce has only months to go.
There will be a party; she will dance, laugh, and sing "Happy
    Birthday" to herself.
We will all gather, my family, her family, and her friends.
We will marvel at all the people that she has birthed.

E. J. Barnett

Why Can't I Touch You

My best friend, though you won't let me in,
I talk to you, shout at you, denounce when you
Don't listen. I laugh with you, share with you,
Moments that are just for us.
But you won't let me in.
You just won't let me in.

I see joy when you're happy.
I see pain when I shout and shun.
I see despair when you witness sadness.
I see concern when I fret and worry,
But you won't let me in.
You just won't let me in.

I can't touch you, though we embrace.
You listen to my thoughts, though yours are silent.
You give your time, your patience, your heart,
Yet it's given anonymously.
You won't let me in.
You just won't let me in.

I sneak a peek whenever I can.
I hide in the crevices of your mind
And I see the joy and that's okay,
I see the laughter and that's okay,
I see the pain, and I beg to come in,
I see confusion and I long to touch you,
You won't let me in.
You just won't let me in.

You are my best friend,
But you shut me out,
You deny my rights to share,
You shun my shoulder, when offered,
You strangle the spirit of the life that's given to you.
You're my best friend, perhaps, one day you'll let me in.

E. J. Barnett

Metamorphosis

In the beginning, he was a man.
Posture perfect, as he walked,
Confident in his thoughts, his movements.
In the beginning, he was a man.

He declared his love in absolutes,
Language that stretched his stature,
Strong, tall, unbending, that of a hu-man.
In the beginning, he was a man.

Years passed, his words grew foreign,
His stature began to shrink,
His thoughts and movements were confusing,
A change had begun.

As time passed, his touch became soft,
Much like that of larvae.
His stature continued to constrict more rapidly
With his unsolicited declarations of love.

Once a call came,
Her voice was soft, she spoke with assurance.
He declared his love as he walked
Towards the door, luggage in hand.

He declared his love,
As his body lost its form,
As he continued to inch towards the door,
Across the floor.

He declared his love,
As he reached the door
And wiggled under,
All backbone ceased to exist.

There were voices outside,
I must protect him
From those that fail to see his new form.
I must. I must.

Approaching the door, I stopped,
Leaned my back against the door.
I smiled, knowing, without backbone, on his level,
He would not reach her in time, to get a spine.

Death

I have started a long journey
Into the world of imprisonment.
I can see in the distance, my hostess,
Holding out her warm arms,
Gleaming eyes,
Fleshy flesh,
Welcoming in my cold, dreary trunk.

When she touches me,
I am not cold.
When she smiles at me,
I feel her warmth
In my sunken, molded face
Of peace.
Warmth, peace, and rest.

My Two Angels

Not long ago, we laughed till the wee hours,
About nothing, just talking, laughing, and playing Scrabble.
It was comforting in knowing, dusk or dawn,
There was no change; the change was in the moments.

My one angel was protective, yet a daredevil.
My shield, my rock, yet my thrill seeker.
Sky diving, river rafting, and introducing me to Harley.
In his presence, I feared only moments passing too quickly.

My other angel was soft spoken and inquisitive, yet he too,
    embraced the untrodden.
Climbing the mountains of China, as well as the great
    northwest.
Writing of his climbs, and sharing the sights, the sounds, and
    the feelings.
He devoured my letters and I consumed each of his.

My one angel shared walks with my canines and me.
Walking in the parks, the four of us,
Some pooping, some scooping, but all enjoying the moments.
Running on the beaches, the four of us,
Allowing the sand to tease our toes before leaving.

My other angel took me to the docks,
Showing me the boats he helped to build.
Standing on the pier, observing the sun's brilliance in the
    water,
Holding hands, talking without words,
Cradling our thoughts and our visions with the water.

67

E. J. Barnett

It was not long ago, one friend chose to leave,
No good-bye; no unspoken words left behind,
It was quick and final and the projectile his means of travel,
Quick, fast, much like he lived, that of a daredevil.

Days later, my other friend chose to leave,
No good-bye, no unspoken words left behind,
He chose to travel the way he lived;
The ropes were strong and tight, much like he climbed.

My two angels left me behind, alone, and torn.
One was my rock, my shield, my lifeline,
The other was my poet, my friend, and my lover.
My two angels, though gone, I wait, I seek the unspoken.

Ghost

There are times that I ache
Knowing I cannot stop
Loving the empty footprints.

I sit staring at the shadows
Of the lucid memories
That shimmers, leaking through cracks.

Crying the tears of silence
Feeling the heat passing
Over hollow skeletal cheeks.

Is there no end?
Will there be a time when
The dust settles and clay appears?

I stand, stretching
To see the darkness part,
Unveiling the image.
In the harmony of joy,
The crimson sparkles
Of the overflowing lust of light.

E. J. Barnett

The Sacred Baton

There are seventeen,
Four couples plus five
I am sitting with three others;
The table is long, cold and dividing.
The five have offspring being watched
By someone to help to observe, to listen.

One is fighting breast cancer; weeks remain before she is
  defeated.
Another must surrender when the tumor in her brain declares
  victory.
A wayward lover, without conscious, bestowed the AIDS virus
  on another.
The fourth was a runner until ovarian cancer challenged.
In her youth, another gave a kidney, now the other is shutting
  down.
The five began to talk, to share.

The couples are silent, alert, listening to the three.
They are well-educated professionals in their fields.
There are two lawyers, three doctors, a teacher, an engineer,
  and a pilot
One couple has a daughter; the others have none
They all want to claim the offsprings; they are patient.
The couples are silent, alert, listening to the three.

One mother speaks of Johnny; he is ten, loves the computer
and the violin.
Another, smiles, as she shares the love seven-year-old Sara has
for science.
Three-year-old Clarence loves to draw and finger paint.
Jim and Joe's mother worry that no one will want two twelve
year olds
They are identical twins, active in sports, and in love with
camping.
Jack is eight; he reads and writes to pen-pals in faraway places.

A break is given; the five stand and approach the windows.
The eight, slowly stand, then they too, approach the windows.
The three talk amongst themselves, but watching all
I stand, I mingle with the couples, and I mingle with the
mothers.
As I approach the window, I see the children playing, what
appears to be "catch"
The ball is tossed, but not caught; the eyes cannot see without
the mind.
The children walk to retrieve what was missed, what was not
seen in passing
The eyes are blank, methodical in their actions, faces without
smiles
As I stare out, one child turns to look in.
Another, stops the pretense, turns toward the window then
smiles
Soon, all the children are smiling; laughing and their eyes are
dancing
They run to the windows, they run to their mothers, they run to
life.

The break is over, seats are taken, and the children are in
    another room
Each mother in turn, tells a bit of her history and a bit of her
    child's.
She shares her desires for the future of her child
Each mother in turn, shares the amount of time she has.
She speaks of her fears, her child's fears, and their good-byes.
Each mother cries for her pain and each of the other mother's
    pain.

The couples are weeping amongst themselves, and with the
    mothers
Across the tables, they reach out to the mothers, squeezing
    their hands
The couples stand at various times, unable to contain
    themselves
Reaching out with their souls for the dying souls
The counselors are listening, watching, and writing
I see and feel the tragedy; I see the joy ahead.
The mother's are passing their clay to the couples,
To complete the completion of God's Masterpiece.

Faith

So easy to give,
So difficult to keep.